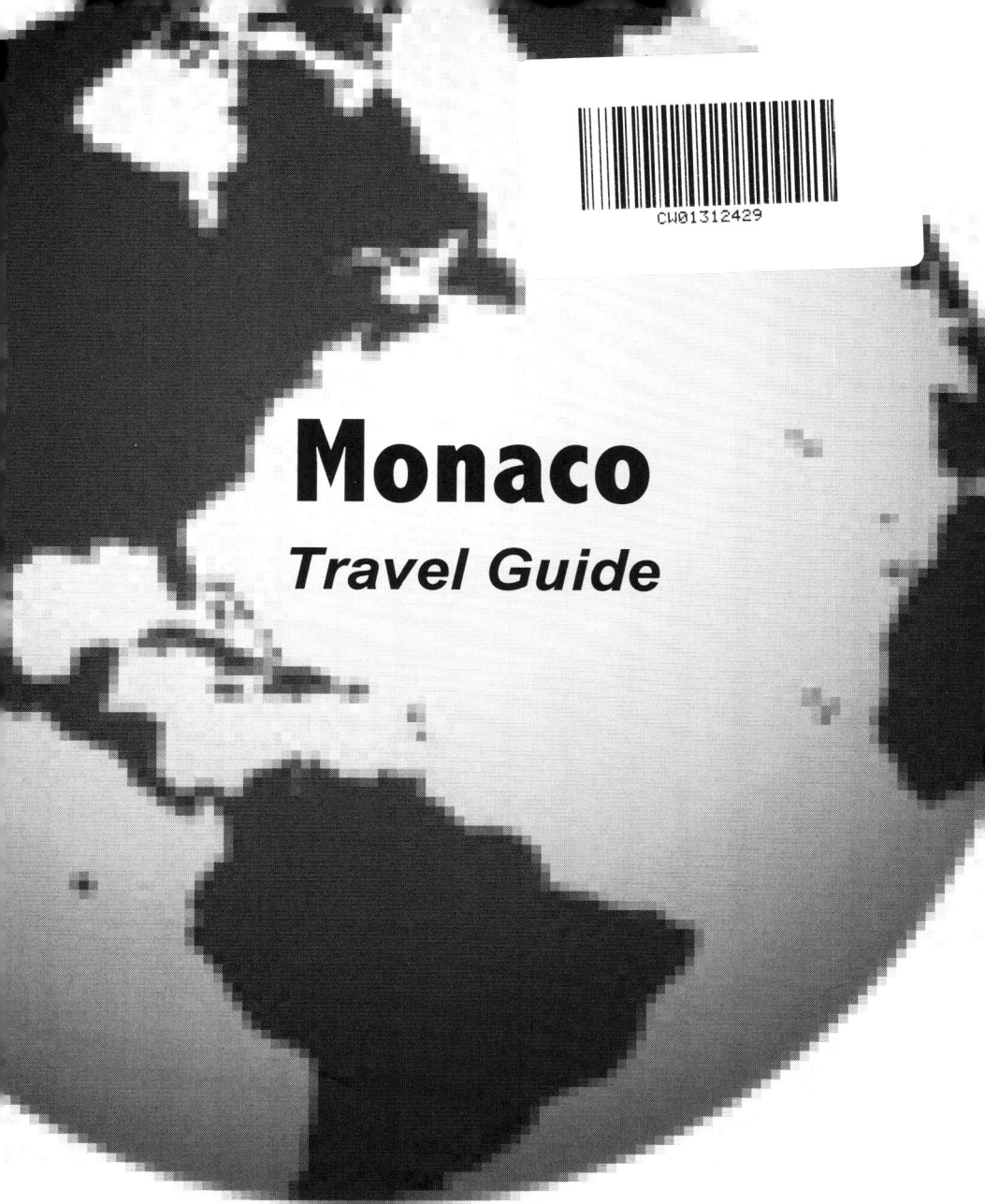

Monaco
Travel Guide

Quick Trips Series

No part of this publication may be reproduced, stored in a retrieval system, or transmitted, in any form or by any means without the prior written permission of the publisher, nor be otherwise circulated in any form of binding or cover other than that in which it is published and without similar condition being imposed on the subsequent purchaser. If there are any errors or omissions in copyright acknowledgements the publisher will be pleased to insert the appropriate acknowledgement in any subsequent printing of this publication. Although we have taken all reasonable care in researching this book we make no warranty about the accuracy or completeness of its content and disclaim all liability arising from its use.

Copyright © 2016, Astute Press
All Rights Reserved.

Table of Contents

MONACO 6
- 🌐 GEOGRAPHY..9
- 🌐 WEATHER & BEST TIME TO VISIT 10

SIGHTS & ACTIVITIES: WHAT TO SEE & DO 12
- 🌐 CATHEDRAL OF MONACO 12
- 🌐 COLLECTION DES VOITURES ANCIENNES DE LE PRINCE 13
- 🌐 JARDIN EXOTIQUE 15
- 🌐 LES GRANDS APPARTEMENTS DU PALAIS 16
- 🌐 MUSEE OCEANOGRAPHIQUE DE MONACO 17
- 🌐 NOUVEAU MUSEE NATIONAL DE MONACO 19
- 🌐 CASINO GARDENS CABARET 20
- 🌐 PRINCESS ANTOINETTE PARK 21
- 🌐 CASINO GARDENS AND TERRACES 22
- 🌐 JAPANESE GARDEN 22
- 🌐 ST. MARTIN GARDENS 23
- 🌐 ZOOLOGICAL GARDENS 24
- 🌐 PRINCESS GRACE ROSE GARDEN & FONTVIEILLE PARK.......25
- 🌐 MUSEUM OF NAPOLEONIC SOUVENIRS & HISTORICAL ARCHIVES 26
- 🌐 NAVAL MUSEUM 27
- 🌐 OPERA HOUSE 28

- Monte Carlo Casino 29
- Sainte Dévote Church 30
- Fort Antoine Theater 31
- Circuit de Monaco 32
- Grimaldi Forum 32
- Marlborough Fine Arts Gallery 33
- Larvotto Beach 34

BUDGET TIPS 36

- Accommodation 36
  - Columbus Monte Carlo Hotel 36
  - Fairmont Monte Carlo 37
  - Hôtel Capitole 38
  - Hôtel Hermitage 39
  - Hotel Metropole 40
- Shopping 41
  - Marché de la Condamine 41
  - Marché de Monte Carlo 42
- Places to Eat 43
  - Cosmopolitan 43
  - Cafe Llorca 44
  - Zest 45
  - Huit et Demi 45
  - Tip Top 46
  - Alextony 46
  - Maciota 47

KNOW BEFORE YOU GO 49

- Entry Requirements 49
- Health Insurance 50
- Travelling with Pets 50

- 🌐 **AIRPORTS** 51
- 🌐 **AIRLINES** 53
- 🌐 **CURRENCY** 54
- 🌐 **BANKING & ATMS** 54
- 🌐 **CREDIT CARDS** 55
- 🌐 **TOURIST TAXES** 55
- 🌐 **RECLAIMING VAT** 56
- 🌐 **TIPPING POLICY** 56
- 🌐 **MOBILE PHONES** 57
- 🌐 **DIALLING CODE** 58
- 🌐 **EMERGENCY NUMBERS** 58
- 🌐 **TIME ZONE** 59
- 🌐 **DAYLIGHT SAVINGS TIME** 59
- 🌐 **SCHOOL HOLIDAYS** 59
- 🌐 **DRIVING LAWS** 60
- 🌐 **DRINKING LAWS** 61
- 🌐 **SMOKING LAWS** 61
- 🌐 **ELECTRICITY** 62
- 🌐 **FOOD & DRINK** 62

MONACO TRAVEL GUIDE

Monaco

Adjacent to the French Riviera in the South of France, the small, exclusive country of Monaco offers a touch of elegance and a taste of the high life. Monaco has elegant hotels, world-class casinos, captivating gardens, museums and shopping centers. Everything that the rich and famous look for is here. Monte Carlo is also known for its world-famous events such as the Tennis Masters Series, Formula 1 Grand Prix and the Monte Carlo Rally.

MONACO TRAVEL GUIDE

Monaco (derived from the Greek word "Monoikos") is a small European country located between France and the Mediterranean Sea. It has four major areas. Monte Carlo is the administrative seat. La Condamine is adorned by luxurious yachts and an extensive harbor. Fontvieille features a heliport and Monaco Ville is also known as *The Rock*.

With its port lined with expensive yachts, it's easy to see that luxury is a common theme in Monaco. But there are activities for all budgets here and the country features an enticing seaside which gives tourists a chance to stroll to enjoy the sunshine and the breeze. This seaside is a perfect spot to enjoy local cafés and to watch the beautiful people in gorgeous surroundings. The Princess Grace

MONACO TRAVEL GUIDE

Rose Garden offers another option for a scenic stroll with its 4000 rose varieties.

The country has only 30,000 inhabitants composed of various groups in particular the Monegasque, French and Italian. A majority of the people are Roman Catholics and religion has been a main factor in shaping the country's culture. Various feast days are celebrated all over the country like Easter and the Feast Days of Saint John, Saint Roman and Saint Blaise, all packed with rituals and ceremonies.

Even in Monaco's Independence Day, celebrated every 19th of November, Catholicism is apparent. Independence Day features parades, special events and mass, all strongly featuring the church. Protestantism,

MONACO TRAVEL GUIDE

Judaism, Islam, Anglican and Greek Orthodox religions are also widely practiced throughout the country.

The proximity to France and Italy inspires Monaco's culture including its food, feativals, rituals, and languages. Monaco is brimming with restaurants that offer high quality and traditional cuisines. If you're searching for local cuisine then try fougasse (pastry), barbagiuan (pastry), socca (pancakes) or stocafi (dried cod in tomato sauce).

You can taste them at any time and in particular during the Carnivals before Christmas, Lent and Easter. The visitor to Monaco should also try some of the delicious seafood and French wines readily available in most restaurants.

MONACO TRAVEL GUIDE

🌍 Geography

Monaco is a small country which measures just 1.95 kilometers in area (0.75 square miles). Although small, Monaco is an independent country situated right next door to the French Riviera (Cote d'Azur). Monaco's topography is steep-sloped and rugged, and the country has been modernized through time.

Monaco has 31 miles of cemented roads and highways, and 1.1 miles of railroads which connect Southern France through Monaco to Italy. Monaco has two ports which include merchant harbors and marinas. Air transportation is possible to Monaco by the helicopter shuttle line in the midst of Fontvieille and for everyone else, the Nice international airport close-by in France.

MONACO TRAVEL GUIDE

⊙ Weather & Best Time to Visit

Monaco is lovely in each of the four seasons. Since it is located between the Mediterranean and at the bottom of the Southern Alps, the country enjoys a hot summer and has mild winters. Monaco offers visitors 300 days of sunshine on average per year.

Summertime in Monaco is characterized by 20°C - 23°C temperatures and the water at this time can reach up to 26°C. Monaco averages just two to three days of rainfall during the entire summer. At nighttime, the country enjoys cool evening breezes that come in from the Mediterranean, offering you the perfect temperature to dine by the seafront.

During winter which is from December to February, the

MONACO TRAVEL GUIDE

country registers an average temperature of 9.5°C. During the winter months the ski resorts in the neighboring Southern Alps will beckon.

Spring (April/May) and Autumn (September/October) temperatures range from 15°C to 21°C (averages). At this time, you can enjoy the milder weather and many tourists to Monaco feel these months are the best times to visit the country. This is the temperature to expect when the Formula One Grand Prix is held in the country.

MONACO TRAVEL GUIDE

Sights & Activities: What to See & Do

🌐 Cathedral of Monaco

Av. St-Martin

Tel: 377-93-30-87-70

The Cathedrale de Monaco is a popular sight for visitors as Princess Grace Kelly's tomb can be found here. A lot

MONACO TRAVEL GUIDE

of Monoco's Royal Family have been buried here over the ages. Among them were the Grimaldis and recently Prince Rainier III was buried here.

The Cathedrale de Monaco is an icon of Monaco as it holds a part of its history. It was built on the location of the first ever church in the country which was established in the year 1252.

In 1911, it was venerated and dedicated to the honor of Saint Nicholas. The cathedral features a white Carrara marble altar and a huge organ comprised of 5,000 pipes. During April until October the cathedral is open from 8 in the morning until 7 in the evening. From November to March, Cathedrale de Monaco is open from 8 in the morning until 6 in the evening. Admission is free.

MONACO TRAVEL GUIDE

🌐 Collection des Voitures Anciennes de le Prince

Les Terrasses de Fontvieille

Tel: 377-92-05-28-56

If you love cars as the former prince of Monaco did, this place is a perfect spot for you. It serves as a unique museum for Prince Rainier III's private collection of vintage cars. Among the vintage cars on display are the model 1956 Rolls-Royce Silver Cloud and the Austin Taxi model of 1952.

All cars on display have their own stories to tell. For example the former was the car used in transporting the newlyweds on their wedding day. The latter on the other hand, had been the "royal family car" for many years.

MONACO TRAVEL GUIDE

A 1937 Ford, also known as "woodie", can be found among the collections on display also. This car was used as the official car during the hunting trips of Prince Louis II. On display also is the winner of the 1929 Monaco Grand Prix which is a 1925 Bugatti 35B, the 1903 model of De Dion Bouton and the 1986 model of Lamborghini Countach. For car lovers, this will truly be a feast.

Access to this museum is 6€ for adults. For students and children (aged 8 to 14 years), the fee is 3€. Under-7's can visit for free. The museum is open daily except December 25. You can visit Collection des Voitures Anciennes de S.A.S. le Prince de Monaco from 10 in the morning until 6 in the evening.

MONACO TRAVEL GUIDE

🌐 Jardin Exotique

62, Boulevard du Jardin Exotique

98000 Monaco,

Tel: 377-93-15-29-80

Ever heard of a cactus garden? You may want to see one while in Monaco. Jardin Exotique gives you a display of cacti from the most common to the most exotic kinds. The garden is suitable for cactus growing since it is located in a rocky location.

The cactus collection was started in the 19th century when naturalist and scientist, Prince Albert I observed some unusual plants growing in the palace gardens. He built a garden for them and in 1933 the Jardin Exotique was opened to the public. In this place you can also visit the Musee d'Anthropologie Prehistorique.

The garden gives a stunning view of the principality. You can visit from mid-May to mid-September from 9 in the morning to 7 in the evening. It is open to the public for 7€ for adults. Children from 6 to 18 years of age costs 3.70€. Children aged under 5 can visit free of charge.

🌐 Les Grands Appartements du Palais

Place du Palais

Tel: 377-93-25-18-31

Artwork of the rich and items used by the famous are on display in the Les Grands Appartements du Palais museum. This was the former home of the royal family. It

MONACO TRAVEL GUIDE

was completed in the 13th century and additional parts of the palace were completed during the Renaissance period. Palais Princier de Monaco, as it is also known, houses artworks created by Bruegel and Holbein and has a state portrait of Princess Grace.

You can also see here the Throne Room as well as the musee (Souvenirs Napoleoniens et Archives du Palais) which contain memorabilia of Napoleon. During the time when the royal home is closed, the museum is the only part of this palace that is accessible to the public.

One of the highlights featured in the palace is the Releve de la Garde (the changing of the guard). This happens at 11:55 each morning and the ceremony lasts for about 10 minutes. This is the best time of day to tour the palace.

MONACO TRAVEL GUIDE

The palace and the museum are both open to the public from April to October from 10 in the morning to 6 in the evening. The museum on the other hand is accessible to the public from December to March from 10:35 in the morning until 5 in the afternoon. Tickets costs 8€ for adults, 3.50€ for kids aged 8 to 14 years old while kids 7 years old and under are free.

🌐 Musee Oceanographique de Monaco

Av. St-Martin

Tel: 377-93-15-36-00

Being a naturalist and scientist, Prince Albert's hobby did not stop at just collecting botany. During his research trips, the prince collected various fish and sea creatures

MONACO TRAVEL GUIDE

now on display at the Oceanographique de Monaco museum. It highlights the sub-aqua world, and features a basement aquarium containing sea bass, sea horses and jellyfishes.

You can also see sharks and other marine animals amounting to 90 tanks full. Also showcased in the museum also are models of ships and scientific prototypes that Prince Albert I collected between 1885 and 1915 during his voyages in the Mediterranean and North Atlantic. Also on display are various maritime paintings, sculptures and drawings.

Monaco's Oceanographic Museum was founded in 1910 by Prince Albert I. On its 100th anniversary, it purchased a 150 million years old reptile called Anna. It was also when Huang Yong Ping's beautiful octopus design was added.

You can visit the museum from April to September at 9:30 in the morning until 7 in the evening but from July to August they are open until 7:30 in the evening. During October to March, the museum is open from 10 in the morning until 6 in the evening. For adult visitors a 14€ admission fee is due. For children aged 4 to 18 years of age there is a 7€ admission fee while for kids of three years of age and below, visits to the museum are free.

🌐 Nouveau Musee National de Monaco

56 Blvd. du Jardin Exotique

Tel: 377-93-30-91-26 & 377-98-98-48-60

MONACO TRAVEL GUIDE

The splendid National Museum has now been expanded to two at Villa Paloma and Villa Sauber. It offers the wide range of art from the ancient to the modern as well as a wide array of sculptures, paintings, and other exhibitions.

Villa Sauber mixes arts with fashion and showcases collections of antique toys and dolls. It is great spot to visit with your kids. The Nouveau Musee National de Monaco is open all year from 10 in the morning until 6 in the evening. It costs 6€ admission fee for adults over age 26. Visitors aged under 26 can visit for free.

🌐 Casino Gardens Cabaret

Casino Gardens, Monte Carlo

Tel: 92-16-36-36

MONACO TRAVEL GUIDE

Feathers, jazz, glitter and ballet can all be seen at the Cabaret of Casino Gardens in Monte Carlo. If you want to experience nightlife the Monaco way, this place is the best on offer.

A Riviera-style (semi-nude) show is presented on Tuesday to Sunday in June to September at 10 in the evening. However, if you want to dine as a part of the show, dinner is served at 9 pm at a cost of 75€ per person. If you intend just to see the show with drinks you pay 25.50€.

🌐 Princess Antoinette Park

54 Boulevard du Jardin Exotique

Tel: (0)93 30 92 12

MONACO TRAVEL GUIDE

If you have read Frances Hodgson Burnett's novel The Secret Garden, you will be able to imagine its setting while visiting here. From the wall covered by colourful bougainvillea, you will be entranced as you walk through this dramatic park. Once the venue for royal meetings and their country banquets the park is now open to the public and has free admittance.

🌍 Casino Gardens and Terraces

Place du Casino

Monte Carlo

Tel: +44 (0)207 491 4264

If you want to see a delightful French-themed garden then visit the Casino Gardens and Terraces which is located high on a hill, overlooking the sea. Fountains and verdant lawns abound and the "Little Africa" garden contains a variety of African plants. As you move further downhill, you reach the "Hexa Grace", a hexagonal tiled roof on the convention center designed by Victor Vasarely. Admission is free.

🌐 Japanese Garden

Avenue Princess Grace, Monte Carlo

Tel: 33 (0)377 98 98 22 77

This typical Japanese garden will help you to experience a touch of Asia in Monaco. Complying with Zen principles, the 7000 square metre garden shows balance and harmony in the assembling of its stones, water and vegetation.

MONACO TRAVEL GUIDE

You will find idyllic waterfalls and brooks which will encourage you to relax and unwind. The Japanese Garden is open from 9 in the morning until sunset. Admission is free of charge.

🌎 St. Martin Gardens

2 Avenue Saint-Martin

Tel: +44 (0)207 491 4264

Having wild Mediterranean greenery plus an exuberant display of exotic plants and species, you cannot help but marvel at the display that St. Martin Gardens offers.

As the road winds lazily along a furrow, you can enjoy nature's best along with works of arts and its water features. The St. Martin Gardens are open to all and have free admission.

🌍 Zoological Gardens

Terrasses de Fontvieille

Tel: 377-93-50-40-30

Monaco's Zoological Garden shows off over 250 animals belonging to 50 species. If you are an animal lover, you will surely enjoy observing the animals on display.

The Zoological garden was founded in 1954 by Prince Rainier III and is located on the southern side of the Grimaldi Rock. Adults can tour the zoo for 5€ while for children and students the admission cost is 3€.

MONACO TRAVEL GUIDE

The Zoological Garden is open daily. From October to February it is open from 10 in the morning until 12 noon. It resumes at 2 in the afternoon until 5.

From March to May, you can visit from 9 in the morning until 12 noon and then from 2 in the afternoon until 6. For the months of June to September, it is open at 9 in the morning until 12 noon and 2 in the afternoon until 7.

🌐 Princess Grace Rose Garden & Fontvieille Park

Avenue des Guelfes, Monte Carlo

Tel: +377 92 16 61 16

With over 4 hectares in size, the garden offers contemporary sculptures and nearly 4,000 roses. It is a place of serenity and beauty and is open every day from sunrise until sunset. Free Admission.

🌍 Museum of Napoleonic Souvenirs & Historical Archives

Place du Palais

Monaco Ville

Tel: 377-93-25-18-31

Your stay in Monaco will be complete only after you have peered into its rich history. And you can do just that at this museum. It contains prized items and documents which are vital to the history of Monaco. Most of the articles depict the story of its rulers during the First French Empire.

MONACO TRAVEL GUIDE

The museum is open daily. In December until May it can be visited from 10:30 in the morning until 12:30 in the afternoon and from 2 in the afternoon until 5. During June to September the museum is open from 9:30 in the morning until 6 in the evening. In October it is open to public from 10 in the morning until 5 in the afternoon.

The museum is closed from 12-16 November and on 25th of December as well as 1st of January. A visit to the museum costs 4€ for adults and 2€ for children aged 8 to 14.

🌐 Naval Museum

Terrasses de Fontvieille

Tel: 377-92-05-28-48

MONACO TRAVEL GUIDE

Monaco Naval museum showcases 250 types of marine transportation. The collection ranges from simple boats to intricate vessels as well as the personal collection of Prince Rainier II.

The Naval Museum is open from 10 in the morning until 6 in the evening except on the 25th of December and 1st of January.

Adults can access the museum for 4€ while children aged 8-14 cost 2.50€.

🌐 Opera House

Tel : + 377 98 06 21 21

www.opera.mc

MONACO TRAVEL GUIDE

For an entrance fee of 10 Euros, you can visit the famous opera house in Monaco. The opera house was a creation of the famous architect, Charles Garnier in 1893. It is made of marble, onyx, with red and gold decorations. The fantastic sculptures that lead to the opera hall will delight the visitor.

The opera house stages many concerts, operatic productions and ballet performances from world-renowned performers. Some of the past performers include Dalla Rizza, Caruso, **Chaliapine**, Garden, Gigli, Lubin, Melba, Muzio, Patti, Pons, Schipa, Tamagno and Thill.

The Opera also houses creative works by artists including Lowell Liebermann, Rendine, Massenet, Bizet and

MONACO TRAVEL GUIDE

Franck. It is important to bring proof of identity so that you can enter the opera house. Guided tours last for 40 minutes.

Monte Carlo Casino

Place du Casino

Monte Carlo 98000

Tel: 92 16 20 00

Sophisticated (and well-dressed) tourists are sure to enjoy the elegant atmosphere of the Casino of Monte Carlo and it has a vast terrace that gives the visitor a fantastic view of the ocean below.

It allows players to to play under the romantic night skies, and recalls the days of James Bond, filmed in this very

MONACO TRAVEL GUIDE

Casino decades ago. On display in the historic building are sculptures, exotic plants and palms and this is one of the most famous casinos in the world. Jacket and tie required for entry.

🌐 Sainte Dévote Church

1 Rue Sainte-Dévote 98000 Monaco

(0)93 50 52 60

Chapelle Sainte Dévote is a Roman Catholic chapel dedicated to patron Saint Devote. It was built in 1070 and reconstructed by Prince Honore in 1606. In 1637, a porch was added on the church and from 1870 to 1891, the frontage was rebuilt.

The original glass windows were created by Nicolas Lorin. However, these glass windows were destroyed during the Second World War. In 1948, the windows were restored by Fassi Cadet.

In 1887, Chapelle Sainte Dévote was declared as Monaco's Parish Church. Originally, Chapelle Sainte Dévote was constructed in Vallon des Gaumates where the body of Saint Dévote had been found at its entrance during the 4th century. Every January 26, a burning boat ceremony is conducted to commemorate the event.

🌐 Fort Antoine Theater

Tel: 93 15 80 00

MONACO TRAVEL GUIDE

Fort Antoine is an outdoor theater in Monaco which was established during the Spanish succession war. It was originally built in the 18th century as a fortress and it was rebuilt by 1954 under the patronage of Prince Rainier.

Now, Fort Antoine is one of the most comfortable and well-designed theaters in the world. It has 365 seats which are positioned in semi-circular stepped rows. The theater hosts many performances during summer and on special occasions and the theater does not charge entrance fee to visit when a show is not taking place.

🌐 Circuit de Monaco

23 Boulevard Albert 1er.

BP 364 98000 Monaco

Tel: (+377) 93 15 26 00

MONACO TRAVEL GUIDE

The Circuit de Monaco is the famous street circuit surrounding the principality of Monaco's harbor.

Featured in many movies, it is laid out on the streets of La Condamine and Monte Carlo. Oftentimes it is referred to as Monte Carlo due to a large portion of the circuit being located in Monte Carlo. During the month of May, the circuit is used for the annual Formula One Monaco Grand Prix.

🌐 Grimaldi Forum

98000 Monaco

Tel: 99 99 20 00

MONACO TRAVEL GUIDE

Grimaldi Forum is Monaco's conference centre with 35,000 sqm of floor space. It was boldly constructed on Monaco's fabulous seafront and is surrounded by the wonderful hills of the Principality. It hosts forums, seminars, exhibitions, conferences and product launches as well as many shows and gala dinners.

The entrance and the auditorium's design are exceptional. The Grimaldi Forum also offers two restaurants that you can visit on your visit here whether you come for a trade show or to see a performance.

🌐 Marlborough Fine Arts Gallery

4 Quai Antoine 1er, 98000 Monaco

Tel: 97 70 25 50

The Marlborough Fine Arts Gallery is one of many located in different parts of the world. On display are artistic masterpieces from after the Second World War as well as by contemporary artists. Art work include paintings, sketches, drawings, and other graphic works. There are beautifully designed jewelries, unique potteries, and fantastic sculptures.

🌐 Larvotto Beach

MC 98000 Monaco

Larvotto Beach is a pleasant public beach in Monaco with concrete jetties, a gravel beach with huge boulders along with many bars and restaurants. You can bathe here from June to September and there are special facilities for the

MONACO TRAVEL GUIDE

disabled (including devices to lower a person into the water).

There are trampolines for kids and volleyball for all ages at the eastern part of the beach. Kids will love the wide array of ice cream stands at the beach and there is a fitness gym for the health conscious.

For other exciting water adventures visit the west side of the beach with its water activities including "long plastic sausage", parasailing, windsurfing, and jet-ski rental. Teenagers and young adults can also enjoy rollerblades, bikes and skateboards at the upper level. This public man-made beach is bursting with sun-lovers during the summer so get there early.

MONACO TRAVEL GUIDE

Budget Tips

🌍 Accommodation

Columbus Monte Carlo Hotel

Tel: 377-92-05-90-00

http://www.columbushotels.com/

This is a hotel featuring a fusion of elegance and

MONACO TRAVEL GUIDE

modernity. The owner says the hotel is for the "hybrid hip" as it has a touch of elegance. There are video game filled high tech cabinets. Columbus Monte-Carlo Hotel faces the Princess Grace Garden and the sea which gives breathtaking views from the hotel.

All rooms are furnished with exquisite linens, bathrobes and chocolate-leather furnishings. Liked by guests are the pool, cocktail bar and brasserie.

Additional facilities offered by the hotel are babysitting, concierge, exercise room and room service. Guestrooms have air-conditioning, TV, and a mini bar. A double room price ranges from 160€ to 300€. Their suite on the other hand, starts at 240€.

Fairmont Monte Carlo

Tel: 377-93-50-65-00

http://www.fairmont.com/Montecarlo

The Fairmont Monte Carlo is a four-star hotel. From the history of its architecture, this hotel holds elegance beyond compare. Having a foundation built on a seabed and busy highways underneath, the hotel is a true beauty. It is located just above the famous casino which overlooks the sea and the town.

In 2009, the hotel underwent a 46€ million renovation. Recently added is a spa and rooftop restaurant called Horizon. L'Argentin is the other restaurant that can be found in the hotel. It serves grilled steaks and other

MONACO TRAVEL GUIDE

Argentine cuisine. Rooms are furnished in happy pastel-colored decorations.

Guests will enjoy amenities like air-conditioned rooms, hair dryer, minibar and WiFi connection which can be accessed for 20€/day. Facilities that can be found in this hotel are two restaurants, 2 bars, babysitting, concierge, casino, health club with sauna and room service. A double room costs 365€ to 530€ while the suite costs 1,500€ per person. Monte Carlo is not exactly cheap!

Hôtel Capitole

Tel: 04-93-28-65-65

http://www.hotel-capitole.fr/

Exploring Monaco will not be hard if you will stay in this

central hotel. It is referred to as located on Beausoleil or on "French soil" since it is found on the French side of Monte Carlo.

Rooms range from small to medium in size and overlook the street. In room amenities include air conditioning, television, minibar, and free access to WiFi. Babysitting is offered by this hotel. Room rates range from 115€ to 145€.

Hôtel Hermitage

Tel: 377-98-06-40-00

http://www.hotelhermitagemontecarlo.com/

If you want to experience real comfort away from home, Hotel Hermitage is what you are looking for. With rooms

MONACO TRAVEL GUIDE

having balconies you can also enjoy the sights and sounds below. The main building is a century old but the guestrooms are designed and decorated with modernity in mind. Rooms are furnished with large beds, large mirrors, exquisite bathrooms, and fancy fabrics.

Room amenities include air conditioning, hair dryer, minibar and WiFi that can be accessed for 20€/day. The hotel offers additional facilities such as restaurants, 2 bars, babysitting, concierge, health club and spa, indoor pool and room service. It has direct access to the Thermes Marins spa and health club.

Prices range from 390€ to 1,080€ for a double room, while a junior suite starts from 655€ per person. A suite on the other hand starts from 1,640€ per person.

MONACO TRAVEL GUIDE

Hotel Metropole

Tel: 377-93-15-15-15

http://www.metropole.com/

The Hotel Metropole is located at the central part of the country. It is a five star hotel and is the only five star hotel not owned by the Societe des Baines de Mer.

The hotel features hypoallergenic pillows and a lineup of branded toiletries. Another factor adding to the fame of the hotel is its master chef, Joel Robuchon, who is a two-Michelin-starred-chef. The hotel restaurant offers French, International and Japanese cuisine.

The room amenities include air-conditioning, hair dryer, minibar and free access to WiFi. Additional facilities also include two restaurants, bar, babysitting, concierge, outdoor pool, room service and spa.

The hotel has one of the finest spas in Monaco. Room rates at this hotel range from 290€ to 690€ for a double room while prices start at 490€ for a suite.

🌐 Shopping

Marché de la Condamine

Place d'Armes

Condamine Shopping Area

Phone: (+377) 93 30 63 94

Marché de la Condamine is a shopping haven for budget travelers who want to buy fresh produce, wine, homeware and baked products. You can buy flowers, vegetables and

MONACO TRAVEL GUIDE

fruits at the open-air market. Proceed to the covered market which sells affordable and excellent French wines that will suit your taste.

The covered market has bakeries, fishmongers and butchers. If you're driving you can park for free for the first hour at Parking de la Condamine. Marché de la Condamine is also surrounded by other shopping areas like rue Terrazzani, rue de Millo, rue Princesse Caroline and rue Grimaldi.

If you are too tired to shop or you simply want to enjoy other things while in Condamine, just call Marché de la Condamine's phone number and the town hall can arrange a home delivery service for you from 7:30 am to 2:00PM, daily except Sunday.

MONACO TRAVEL GUIDE

Marché de Monte Carlo

Ave. St-Charles

Phone: (+377) 93 25 46 45

This is a great shopping destination to buy fresh fruits and vegetables while in Monte Carlo. This covered market is open daily and has a covered parking area nearby. Parking is free of charge for the first hour. There are a wide variety of French breads and other delicacies offered at affordable prices.

Fresh meats and dairy products are sold directly by local farmers. You can also shop from the comfort of your hotel room or from any spot in Monte Carlo. You can simply dial the Marché de Monte Carlo's phone number to order your favorite foods, wines, or anything sold in the market.

Delivery service runs daily, excluding Sundays.

🌍 Places to Eat

Cosmopolitan

7 rue du Portier

Monaco 98000

Phone: +377 93 25 78 68

If you love cocktails, wines and excellent international dishes, Cosmopolitan is the place for you. Here you can drink the best selection of New World, French and Italian wines for reasonable prices (although this is Monaco).

Enjoy the soft breeze at the outside seating or enjoy a romantic drink inside in the simple yet elegant atmosphere. If you visit during the winter season, you can taste Cosmopolitan's excellent Sunday roast that will surely please your palate.

Cafe Llorca

10 avenue Princesse Grace

Monaco 98000

Phone: +377 99 99 29 29

Lunchtime menu: 22 Euros

Café Llorca is a lunchtime restaurant that offers sumptuous and affordable dishes. You can also enjoy solitude or time with friends and family on its seaview terrace.

Zest

6 route de la Piscine Monaco 98000

Phone: +377 97 98 49 70

If you're in the mood to party or to simply enjoy a drink while enjoying tasty dishes, visit Zest, a restaurant and a lounge bar that serves French and Italian food. You also enjoy happy hour with friends from Tuesday to Saturday from 5:30 pm to 8 pm.

Huit et Demi

4 rue Langle

Monaco 98000

Phone: +377 93 50 97 02

MONACO TRAVEL GUIDE

Visitors wanting the best regional foods while enjoying lovely music will enjoy Huit et Demi's pavement terrace where you can enjoy the cool breeze while dining or drinking.

Tip Top

11 Avenue des Spelugues

Monaco 98000

Phone: +377 93 50 69 13

If you have partied all night and you want to eat in the morning, Tip Top is the place you are looking for. It serves a variety of meals from full English breakfast to slices of pizza. The prices are inexpensive.

MONACO TRAVEL GUIDE

Alextony

23 Boulevard Princesse Charlotte

Monaco 98000

Phone: +377 97 98 32 62

Alextony is a bar, fast-food and a gourmet food shop that serves pizzas and other Italian dishes using from the finest ingredients from Naples.

Maciota

4 rue Baron de Sainte Suzanne

Monaco 98000

Phone: +377 97 77 14 64

If you are a fan of traditional Italian foods, Maciota Restaurant will satisfy. You can choose from varieties of

MONACO TRAVEL GUIDE

pizzas, pastas and other Italian foods – at budget-friendly prices!

MONACO TRAVEL GUIDE

MONACO TRAVEL GUIDE

Know Before You Go

🌐 Entry Requirements

By virtue of the Schengen agreement, visitors from other countries in the European Union will not need a visa when visiting France. Additionally Swiss visitors are also exempt. Visitors from certain other countries such as Andorra, Canada, the United Kingdom, Ireland, the Bahamas, Australia, the USA, Chile, Costa Rica, Croatia, El Salvador, Guatemala, Honduras, Israel, Malaysia, Mauritius, Monaco, Nicaragua, New Zealand, Panama, Paraguay, Saint Kitts and Nevis, San Marino, the Holy See, Seychelles, Taiwan and Japan do not need visas for a stay of less than 90 days. Visitors to France must be in possession of a valid passport that expires no sooner than three months after the intended stay. UK citizens will not need a visa to enter France. Visitors must provide proof of residence, financial support and the reason for their visit. If you wish to work or study in France, however, you will need a visa.

🌐 Health Insurance

Citizens of other EU countries are covered for emergency health care in France. UK residents, as well as visitors from Switzerland are covered by the European Health Insurance Card

(EHIC), which can be applied for free of charge. Visitors from non-Schengen countries will need to show proof of private health insurance that is valid for the duration of their stay in France (that offers at least €37,500 coverage), as part of their visa application. A letter of coverage will need to be submitted to the French Embassy along with your visa application. American travellers will need to check whether their regular medical insurance covers international travel. No special vaccinations are required.

🌐 Travelling with Pets

France participates in the Pet Travel Scheme (PETS) which allows UK residents to travel with their pets without requiring quarantine upon re-entry. Certain conditions will need to be met. The animal will have to be microchipped and up to date on rabies vaccinations. In the case of dogs, France also requires vaccination against distemper. If travelling from another EU member country, you will need an EU pet passport. Regardless of the country, a Declaration of Non-Commercial Transport must be signed stating that you do not intend to sell your pet. A popular form of travel with pets between the UK and France is via the Eurotunnel, which has special facilities for owners travelling with pets. This includes dedicated pet exercise areas and complimentary dog waste bags. Transport of a pet via this

MONACO TRAVEL GUIDE

medium costs €24. The Calais Terminal has a special Pet Reception Building. Pets travelling from the USA will need to be at least 12 weeks old and up to date on rabies vaccinations. Microchipping or some form of identification tattoo will also be required. If travelling from another country, do inquire about the specific entry requirements for your pet into France and also about re-entry requirements in your own country.

🌐 Airports

There are three airports near Paris where most international visitors arrive. The largest of these is **Charles De Gaulle** (CDG) airport, which serves as an important hub for both international and domestic carriers. It is located about 30km outside Paris and is well-connected to the city's rail network. Most trans-Atlantic flights arrive here. **Orly** (ORY) is the second largest and oldest airport serving Paris. It is located 18km south of the city and is connected to several public transport options including a bus service, shuttle service and Metro rail. Most of its arrivals and departures are to other destinations within Europe. **Aéroport de Paris-Beauvais-Tillé** (BVA), which lies in Tillé near Beauvais, about 80km outside Paris, is primarily used by Ryanair for its flights connecting Paris to Dublin, Shannon Glasgow and other cities.

MONACO TRAVEL GUIDE

There are several important regional airports. **Aéroport Nice Côte d'Azur** (NCE) is the 3rd busiest airport in France and serves as a gateway to the popular French Riviera. **Aéroport Lyon Saint-Exupéry** (LYS) lies 20km east of Lyon and serves as the main hub for connections to the French Alps and Provence. It is the 4th busiest airport of France. **Aéroport de Bordeaux** (BOD) served the region of Bordeaux. **Aéroport de Toulouse – Blagnac** (TLS), which lies 7km from Toulouse, provides access to the south-western part of France. **Aéroport de Strasbourg** (SXB), which lies 10km west of Strasbourg, served as a connection to Orly, Paris and Nice. **Aéroport de Marseille Provence** (MRS) is located in the town of Marignane, about 27km from Marseille and provides access to Provence and the French Riviera. **Aéroport Nantes Atlantique** (NTE) lies in Bouguenais, 8km from Nantes carriers and provides a gateway to the regions of Normandy and Brittany in the western part of France. **Aéroport de Lille** (LIL) is located near Lesquin and provides connections to the northern part of France.

🌀 Airlines

Air France is the national flag carrier of France and in 2003, it merged with KLM. The airline has a Flying Blue rewards program, which allows members to earn, accumulate and

MONACO TRAVEL GUIDE

redeem Flying Blue Miles on any flights with Air France, KLM or any other Sky Team airline. This includes Aeroflot, Aerolineas Argentinas, AeroMexico, Air Europa, Alitalia, China Airlines, China Eastern, China Southern, Czech Airlines, Delta, Garuda Indonesia, Kenya Airways, Korean Air, Middle Eastern Airlines, Saudia, Tarom, Vietnam Airlines and Xiamen Airlines.

Air France operates several subsidiaries, including the low-cost Transavia.com France, Cityjet and Hop! It is also in partnership with Air Corsica. Other French airlines are Corsairfly and XL Airways France (formerly Star Airlines).

France's largest intercontinental airport, Charles de Gaulle serves as a hub for Air France, as well as its regional subsidiary, HOP!. It also functions as a European hub for Delta Airlines. Orly Airport, also in Paris, serves as the main hub for Air France's low cost subsidiary, Transavia, with 40 different destinations, including London, Madrid, Copenhagen, Moscow, Casablanca, Algiers, Amsterdam, Istanbul, Venice, Rome, Berlin and Athens. Aéroport de Marseille Provence (MRS) outside Marseille serves as a hub to the region for budget airlines such as EasyJet and Ryanair. Aéroport Nantes Atlantique serves as a French base for the Spanish budget airline, Volotea.

MONACO TRAVEL GUIDE

🌐 Currency

France's currency is the Euro. It is issued in notes in denominations of €500, €200, €100, €50, €20, €10 and €5. Coins are issued in €2, €1, 50c, 20c, 10c, 5c, 2c and 1c.

🌐 Banking & ATMs

If your ATM card is compatible with the MasterCard/Cirrus or Visa/Plus networks and configured for a 4-digit PIN, you will have no problem drawing money in France. Most French ATMs have an English language option. Remember to inform your bank of your travel plans before you leave. Keep an eye open around French ATMs to avoid pickpockets or scammers.

🌐 Credit Cards

Credit cards are frequently used throughout France, not just in shops, but also to pay for metro tickets, parking tickets, and motorway tolls and even to make phone calls at phone booths. MasterCard and Visa are accepted by most vendors. American Express and Diners Club are also accepted by the more tourist oriented businesses. Credit cards issued in Europe are smart cards that that are fitted with a microchip and require a PIN for each transaction. This means that a few ticket machines, self-service vendors and other businesses may not be configured to accept the older magnetic strip credit cards.

🌐 Tourist Taxes

All visitors to France pay a compulsory city tax or tourist tax ("taxe de séjour"), which is payable at your accommodation. Children are exempt from tourist tax. The rate depends on the standard of accommodation, starting with €0.75 per night for cheaper establishments going up to €4, for the priciest options. Rates are, of course, subject to change.

🌐 Reclaiming VAT

If you are not from the European Union, you can claim back VAT (or Value Added Tax) paid on your purchases in France. The VAT rate in France is 20 percent on most goods, but restaurant goods, food, transport and medicine are charged at lower rates. VAT can be claimed back on purchases of over €175 from the same shop, provided that your stay in France does not exceed six months. Look for shops that display a "Tax Free" sign. The shop assistant must fill out a form for reclaiming VAT. When you submit it at the airport, you can expect your refund to be debited within 30 to 90 days to your credit card or bank account. It can also be sent by cheque.

MONACO TRAVEL GUIDE

🌍 Tipping Policy

In French restaurants, a 15 percent service charge is added directly to your bill and itemized with the words *service compris* or "tip included". This is a legal requirement for taxation purposes. If the service was unusually good, a little extra will be appreciated. In an expensive restaurant where there is a coat check, you may add €1 per coat. In a few other situations, a tip will be appreciated. You can give an usherette in a theatre 50 cents to €1, give a porter €1 per bag for helping with your luggage or show your appreciation for a taxi driver with 5-10 percent over the fare. It is also customary to tip a hair dresser or a tour guide 10 percent.

🌍 Mobile Phones

Most EU countries, including France uses the GSM mobile service. This means that most UK phones and some US and Canadian phones and mobile devices will work in France. While you could check with your service provider about coverage before you leave, using your own service in roaming mode will involve additional costs. The alternative is to purchase a French SIM card to use during your stay in France. France has four mobile networks. They are Orange, SFR, Bouygues Telecom and Free. In France, foreigners are barred

MONACO TRAVEL GUIDE

from applying for regular phone contract and the data rates are somewhat pricier on pre-paid phone services than in most European countries. You will need to show some form of identification, such as a passport when you make your purchase and it can take up to 48 hours to activate a French SIM card. If there is an Orange Boutique nearby, you can buy a SIM for €3.90. Otherwise, the Orange Holiday package is available for €39.99. Orange also sells a 4G device which enables your own portable Wi-Fi hotspot for €54.90. SFR offers a SIM card, simply known as le card for €9.99. Data rates begin at €5 for 20Mb.

🌐 Dialling Code

The international dialling code for France is +33.

🌐 Emergency Numbers

All emergencies: (by mobile) 112
Police: 17
Medical Assistance: 15
Fire and Accidents: 18
SOS All Emergencies (hearing assisted: 114)
Visa: 0800 90 11 79
MasterCard: 0800 90 13 87
American Express: 0800 83 28 20

Public Holidays

MONACO TRAVEL GUIDE

1 January: New Year's Day (Nouvel an / Jour de l'an / Premier de l'an)

March - April: Easter Monday (Lundi de Pâques)

1 May: Labor Day (Fête du Travail / Fête des Travailleurs)

8 May: Victory in Europe Day (Fête de la Victoire)

May: Ascension Day (Ascension)

May: Whit Monday (Lundi de Pentecôte)

14 July: Bastille Day (Fête nationale)

15 August: Assumption of Mary (L'Assomption de Marie)

1 November: All Saints Day (La Toussaint)

11 November: Armistace Day (Armistice de 1918)

25 December: Christmas Day (Noël)

Good Friday and St Stephens Day (26 December) are observed only in Alsace and Moselle.

🌍 Time Zone

France falls in the Central European Time Zone. This can be calculated as Greenwich Mean Time/Co-ordinated Universal Time (GMT/UTC) +2; Eastern Standard Time (North America) -6; Pacific Standard Time (North America) -9.

MONACO TRAVEL GUIDE

🌐 Daylight Savings Time

Clocks are set forward one hour on the last Sunday of March and set back one hour on the last Sunday of October for Daylight Savings Time.

🌐 School Holidays

The academic year in France is from the beginning of September to the end of June. The long summer holiday is from the beginning of July to the end of August. There are three shorter vacation periods. All schools break up for a two week break around Christmas and New Year. There are also two week breaks in February and April, but this varies per region, as French schools are divided into three zones, which take their winter and spring vacations at different times.

🌐 Driving Laws

The French drive on the ride hand side of the road. If you have a non-European driving licence, you will be able to use it in France, provided that the licence is valid and was issued in your country of residence before the date of your visa application. There are a few other provisions. The minimum driving age in France is 18. Your licence will need to be in French or alternately, you must carry a French translation of your driving permit with you.

In France, the speed limit depends on weather conditions. In dry weather, the speed limit is 130km per hour for highways, 110km per hour for 4-lane expressways and 90km per hour for 2 or 3-lane rural roads. In rainy weather, this is reduced to 110km, 100km and 80km per hour respectively. In foggy weather with poor visibility, the speed limit is 50km per hour on all roads. On urban roads, the speed limit is also 50km per hour.

By law, French drivers are obliged to carry a breathalyser in their vehicle, but these are available from most supermarkets, chemists and garages for €1. The legal limit is 0.05, but for new drivers who have had their licence for less than three years, it is 0.02. French motorways are called autorouts. It is illegal in France to use a mobile phone while driving, even if you have a headset.

🌐 Drinking Laws

The legal drinking age in France is 18. The drinking policy regarding public spaces will seem confusing to outsiders. Each municipal area imposes its own laws. In Paris, alcohol consumption is only permitted in licensed establishments. It is strictly forbidden in parks and public gardens.

🌐 Smoking Laws

From 2007, smoking has been banned in indoor spaces such as schools, government buildings, airports, offices and factories in France. The ban was extended in 2008 to hospitality venues such as restaurants, bars, cafes and casinos. French trains have been smoke free since December 2004.

🌐 Electricity

Electricity: 220-240 volts

Frequency: 50 Hz

Electricity sockets in France are unlike those of any other country. They are hermaphroditic, meaning that they come equipped with both prongs and indents. When visiting from the UK, Ireland, the USA or even another European country, you will need a special type of adaptor to accommodate this. If travelling from the USA, you will also need a converter or step-down transformer to convert the current to to 110 volts, to avoid damage to your appliances. The latest models of many laptops, camcorders, mobile phones and digital cameras are dual-voltage with a built in converter.

🌍 Food & Drink

France is a paradise for dedicated food lovers and the country has a vast variety of well-known signature dishes. These include foie gras, bouillabaisse, escargots de Bourgogne, Coq au vin, Bœuf Bourguignon, quiche Lorraine and ratatouille. A great budget option is crêpes or pancakes. Favorite sweets and pastries include éclairs, macarons, mille-feuilles, crème brûlée and croissants.

The country is home to several world-famous wine-growing regions, including Alsace, Bordeaux, Bourgogne, Champagne, Corse, Côtes du Rhône, Languedoc-Roussillon, Loire, Provence and Sud-Ouest and correctly matching food to complimentary wine choices is practically a science. Therein lies the key to enjoying wine as the French do. It accompanies the meal. Drinking wine when it is not lunch or dinner time is sure to mark you as a foreigner. Pastis and dry vermouth are popular aperitifs and favorite after-dinner digestifs include cognac, Armagnac, calvados and eaux de vie. The most popular French beer is Kronenbourg, which originates from a brewery that dates back to 1664.

Websites

http://www.rendezvousenfrance.com/
http://www.france.com/

MONACO TRAVEL GUIDE

http://www.francethisway.com/

http://www.france-voyage.com/en/

http://www.francewanderer.com/

http://wikitravel.org/en/France

http://www.bonjourlafrance.com/index.aspx